TIMES AND PLACES

A Glimpse of Life on the Virginia Peninsula

By Allan C. Hanrahan

TIMES AND PLACES

A Glimpse of Life on the Virginia Peninsula

By Allan C. Hanrahan

To John and Lisa,
This glimpse of a corner of Virginia comes with Best Wishes to You Both — for now and always.

Uncle Allan

Allan C. Hanrahan

PARKE PRESS

Norfolk, Virginia

Design by Marshall Rouse McClure

PUBLISHED BY
PARKE PRESS
Norfolk, Virginia

www.parkepress.com

ISBN 978-0-9883969-1-3

Library of Congress Control Number is available upon request

Printed in the United States of America

Dedicated to my wife, Renee,
and our sons, Gary and Gregory.

FOREWORD | *It was back in the Sixties* when I began doing pen-and-ink sketches in Southeast Virginia, around Newport News, Hampton and Williamsburg, as well as in York County.

The times were turbulent then but the challenge of solving a building's perspective, or capturing a cityscape, provided respite from the radio, television set or newspaper.

Originally, I did the drawings to illustrate articles written for the *Daily Press*'s Sunday magazine *The New Dominion*. Editor Mr. Howard Goshorn was an artist, so the pieces were accepted a bit more readily than usual, and in publishing my work he encouraged me immensely. The "Editor's Notes" are his, and except for the words and drawings in the Afterwords, all of the copy and drawings are as they were in *The New Dominion* magazine.

After *The New Dominion* magazine ceased to exist I continued to do an occasional drawing.

Later, at my wife Renee's urging, I arranged to have many of the drawings printed individually and offered for sale.

Over the years an elderly friend, Mrs. Elizabeth Russell of Exmore (on the Eastern Shore of Virginia) encouraged me to put all my articles and drawings into a book. I procrastinated, and now Mrs. Russell is gone, but perhaps she is looking down with approval of my effort.

And of each reader, I wish the same.

My placement of the material in this work is by design in some cases; in others it is somewhat arbitrary. Because I received invaluable drafting instruction from such gentlemen as Messrs. Lyeth and Erickson at Newport News High School (NNHS), which no longer exists, I decided to place that piece first.

I also took a semester of art at NNHS but I experienced little encouragement from the teacher, and because I was oftentimes more interested in talking to the girls in the class, especially on outside art excursions, not much came of that exposure to art.

To digress, there was a curious contrast between the drafting or mechanical drawing instructors that I encountered and the art teachers. With one humorous exception, the drafting teachers were encouraging and supportive. That exception was a teacher in the National Aeronautics and Space Administration Apprentice School who almost always considered the first solution-drawing turned in to be the correct one, and it took an inordinate amount of self-confidence and effort to convince him otherwise. But he was fine, otherwise; and likewise, the instructors at The College of William and Mary – VPI Extension in Norfolk (now Old Dominion University). However, like the old Harry Chapin tune about the teacher brainwashing the child about his artistic expression, most of the "art" teachers that I have encountered personally have not left me with fond memories. There was that teacher in elementary school, for example, who made me stay after school and draw and redraw and recolor a picture, continually telling me it was wrong. To this day I don't know why, because the hour became late and she just told me to go home. And in addition to the aforementioned elementary school teacher, there was the high-school-level night school teacher, quite condescending, who seemed more interested in affecting a droll sense of humor (at the expense of others) than in encouraging novice artists. His follow-on, however – now that I think about it – was an okay guy. But he was an exception.

In another category was that art history professor at Christopher Newport College (now University) who enhanced my appreciation and knowledge of art, awarded me straight "A's," but who once spoke of me in salty terms.

At the beginning of this Introduction I wrote about placement of the material. Because I led off with NNHS, I followed that with a piece about other old schools in Newport News. Other drawings are grouped by category as well.

The Victory Arch segment is followed by the Hampton National Cemetery monument piece because they were both done in observance of Memorial Day, but a few years apart.

I decided to present the published articles as they initially appeared, with an Afterword to render the material relevant to modern times, with any later or complementary information or drawings included.

Allan C. Hanrahan
July, 2013

TABLE OF CONTENTS

Reunion – Class Of '55

June 15, 1975

Two decades ago, when this sprawling and imposing knowledge dispenser was already thirty-one years old and was the Newport News High School instead of the Newport News Intermediate School that it is at present, a class of graduates, clutching diplomas, walked out on a warm June evening to whatever the future portended.

A plethora of works have been produced about that generation. Films such as "American Graffiti" and "The Last Picture Show;" songs like "American Pie" by Don McLean and "Yesterday Once More" sung by the Carpenters; television shows; short stories by various writers and books by such authors as J. D. Salinger and Jack Kerouac.

Jack Kerouac is long dead now and so are some other personalities of the Fifties, like Dwight Eisenhower, the President; Buddy Holly, the singer; and James Dean, the actor.

The films and television shows have generated a certain amount of nostalgia for those years, leading one product to comment that "it is somewhat disconcerting to be on the sunny side of forty and have your adolescent years considered 'nostalgia'."

In retrospect, and speaking of them as a generation, they did indeed live through "happy days" as one situation comedy television show by that name describes them – however distortingly. The graduates of that class of a score years ago were born during the Great Depression and reared with that economic debacle and the calamity of World War II as backdrops for the unassuming formality and "peace and prosperity" of their age; materialism was another trait of the times.

They were fortunate in particular ways. They were too young for Korea and for the most part were too old for Vietnam; the misuse of drugs was not yet in vogue; and it was not yet necessary for

Newport News High School, 1975

parents of young adults to endure the trauma of their offsprings' new morality. Concurrently, parental permissiveness was not yet the rule.

The graduates of '55 had departed childhood and entered their teens at the beginning of the Fifties and by the end of the decade they were adults; many were married with children of their own.

Now, after twenty years that have seen some unbelievable events, that class – the present young "establishment" – will celebrate its first reunion on June 21 at a picnic in the afternoon and dinner-dance in the evening.

They will reminisce, of course. But to look back does not denote a desire to go back, for the past only serves as prologue. The present is where living must be done.

UPDATE | *June, 1995*   Some 20 years later, the observer stands again in front of that enduring, imposing building, thinking of 1955.

He thinks of how those years of adolescence, when people mature from childhood to adulthood, are unique, and people who have shared those years have a special bond with one another – and a bond with special others: the teachers and administrators who taught and guided them.

He thinks of 1975, the reunion, and the changes that have taken place in the world.

Then, he thinks of 1995, and this world in which we live, and what has occurred in our respective lives. Most of us, like the old school building, have survived; some have not.

So, we gaze at the generations following, consider the present as precious, and see tomorrow as a gift.

The building still stands, now used by the United States Navy as a residence hall for Navy personnel assigned to whatever ship is undergoing construction or overhaul at the Shipyard. Its name is now

Huntington Hall, and with all new windows the facade is decidedly different.

There was a conscientious effort by many old alumni to name one of the new high schools Newport News High School, but that effort failed. Later, many began to withdraw from that viewpoint; after all, there was only one NNHS. It can never be duplicated nor replicated, so let it be, decided many.

July, 2004   The Newport News High School building still exists, still used by the U.S. Navy.

UPDATE
40th Reunion

At this time Navy personnel assigned to the nuclear-powered aircraft carrier USS *Dwight D. Eisenhower* are moving out and on to their ship, but will be replaced in early 2005 by crew members assigned to the USS *George Washington*. Reportedly, they will be followed by crew members of the USS *Carl Vinson*, which will arrive in late 2005 for its own midlife overhaul and refueling.

August, 2008   The 50th Reunion was a success, so I'm told; this class member did not attend. But I did begin attending the monthly lunch gatherings this year.

July, 2009   The Newport News High School building still exists, still used by the U.S. Navy, presently housing many who will be sailing on the aircraft carrier *George H. W. Bush*.

February, 2011   The Newport News High School building still exists, still used by the U.S. Navy. And because construction has just begun on the as yet unnamed aircraft carrier, CVN-79, the grand old building will exist for the foreseeable future.

UPDATE
*50th Reunion
minus one year*

NEWPORT NEWS HIGH SCHOOL

Reunion - Class Of 1956

October 20-21, 2006

THE GIRLS
OF THE
ROCK & ROLL

Elvis has left the building...

The building was the downtown Paramount Theatre, now consigned to oblivion, but in the early spring of 1956 it pulsated with the music and gyrations of a young Elvis Presley, and among the throng of teenagers were many of the girls of the Newport News High School (NNHS) Class of '56 – the girls of the rock & roll.

After the show, Elvis crossed over bustling Washington Avenue to an appliance store that sold phonograph records where he autographed the records put out on his label, and kissed all the young ladies who asked him.

It was such experiences as this that forged a lifelong bond among so many of the girls of the class of '56, the girls of the rock & roll.

Of course, though he would become the "king," Elvis was not the only music man of that era. The signature song of Bill Haley and the Comets, "Rock Around the Clock," would become the de facto theme song of the latter Fifties and, prophetically, one girl of '56 and her boyfriend had already made it "their song."

In a few months the girls would graduate and their boyfriends would go to work in the shipyard, federal civil service, the city treasurer's office, or retail. Some young men would go into the armed forces; it was, after all, a relatively peaceful time, with the Korean conflict three years past.

The girls, too, would get jobs: in civil service, at Noland & Co., and at various retail establishments, and a few would enroll in nursing schools.

Some, just like the boys, would go to college, most for only a year or two, because most would marry young – probably as young as at any time in the nation's history – and begin having babies.

Films and television shows have generated a certain amount of nostalgia for those years: the Fifties; the Eisenhower years; the years between the wars.

Like the Class of 1955 before them, they did indeed live through "happy days." The graduates of that class of 1956 were born during the Great Depression and reared with that economic debacle and the calamity of World War II as backdrops for the unassuming formality and "peace and prosperity" of their age.

The graduates of '56 had departed childhood and entered their teens early in the Fifties and by the end of the decade they were adults; many were married and soon would have children of their own. But they were never far away from the "rock & roll."

However, there is something unique about the girls of the NNHS Class of '56. Always there has remained that large, loosely formed group, or cadre, of girls – now mature women – that refused to let the bonds of adolescence stretch to the breaking point. It is not a clique by any means; it is too inclusive for that. Any girl in the class is welcome to join the rest at the monthly get-together. And all are welcomed. Whether it be at a breakfast in Newport News or Hampton, or at a luncheon in Poquoson, Smithfield, or Williamsburg.

The time and place of such gatherings are publicized by word-of-mouth, and if someone, for some reason, is not notified, then they know who to contact to find out. The system works, and the meetings go on: times to learn of triumphs and tragedies; to whom to send get-well cards or flowers of condolences; and who may need prayers offered for them.

There are evening socials twice a year, in June and December, when the men in the class and husbands – or boyfriends – are invited as well.

There are some key members. But to mention some, would be at the risk of leaving out others, inadvertently.

And now many of them – the girls of the rock & roll – are involved in planning their class's Fifty-fifth Reunion, set for 2011.

Soon There Will Be Nothing But Memories Left

May 12, 1972

"School days, school days; dear old 'Golden Rule' days," goes the familiar refrain, and gone or going are the old schools themselves, victims of age and obsolescence. Still, they served a purpose – they filled a need – and generations of often-unwilling students marched through their interiors and departed with a little knowledge and a little wisdom miraculously tucked away inside their little craniums.

The four former schools shown are not all of the old school buildings in Newport News; others are still in use, e. g. Hilton (1919), P. L. Dunbar (1924), Woodrow Wilson (prior to 1927), and part of Stonewall Jackson (1902), which incidentally is along the lines of "old" Magruder. And Walter Reed (1918), located at Twenty-fifth Street and Wickham Avenue, has only recently been retired, transferred to the City of Newport News, and presently planned as a multi-purpose neighborhood facility for the East End of the city. A federal grant from the Department of Housing and Urban Development has already been applied for.

"SCHOOL DAYS"

However, of the four schools shown, one is gone, another will soon be gone and for a third the future is uncertain. Only the "old" Magruder School building seems destined for extended future use.

Following is a brief history of the schools pictured: red-brick reminders of a more placid era in education.

Bankhead Magruder School

This building looked massive to this writer when he was a six-year-old seeing it for the first time on a sunny September morning nearly thirty years ago. And he has memories of the quaint "rainy-day sessions" (remember those?) and walking to that house of learning through a gauzy envelope of fog when all the world was seen as myriad shades of grey and the school loomed up out of the mist, lighted and welcoming.

Named for the Virginia General of the War Between The States, the Bankhead Magruder School at 1141 Twenty-second Street was built in 1902 to serve the elementary grades and was discontinued as a school in 1948 upon the completion of the new Magruder School at Seventeenth Street and Chestnut Avenue. The "old" Magruder School was later converted to use as the headquarters of the School Administration.

Since 1966 the building has served as the Title I center; Title I being the Federal program of aid – in matters affecting education – to children of families whose income is considered below the poverty level.

Named for – well, that's obvious – this school is located at 821 Twenty-eighth Street and was built in 1899. It was discontinued as an elementary school in 1941 and for the next five years served as a vocational school under an agreement between the Federal Government and the Newport News Shipyard. Purchased by organized labor in 1947, it at one time housed the unions of the plumbers and steam-fitters, electricians, painters, laborers, and carpenters and joiners, but now its only tenant is Local 396 of the Carpenters and Joiners Union, the other trades having moved out to other quarters. This building is "on the market" so its future is uncertain.

George Washington School

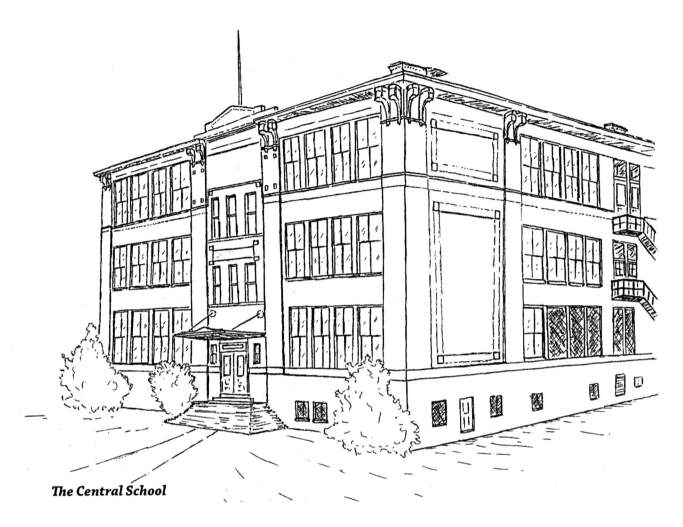

The Central School

The Central School at 222 Thirty-second Street was built in 1899 and served as both an elementary and high school. In 1908 it was renamed the John H. Daniel School after the disabled Confederate veteran who served as U.S. Senator from Virginia during the years 1887 to 1910.

In June of 1913 it caught fire and burned but was rebuilt and back in use by December, 1914.

Then, in September of 1918, the high school classes were transferred to Walter Reed, completed just the previous May.

Discontinued as an elementary school in 1961, the Daniel School building served as the original home of the Christopher Newport

The Boys' School

College for three years, and after the College moved to its new facilities on Shoe Lane the building housed parts of the School Administration. On November 1, 1971, the building was transferred from the School Administration to the City of Newport News and is slated for demolition in the early Spring, although at this writing no contract has been let or date set.

The Boys' School (or the Brothers' School), named after the Xaverian Brothers who organized it, was built in 1902 at the southwest corner of Thirty-fifth Street and Virginia Avenue (now Warwick Boulevard) at a cost of $60,000. The building served the boys of the St. Vincent's Parochial (Catholic) School until around 1931 when the Boys' School and Girls' Schools were merged in the present Peninsula Catholic High School building. The elementary school classes were terminated in June, 1969.

    After 1931 the "Brothers' School" building was vacant until purchased by the Knights of Columbus around 1939. Over the years it became known as the "K of C" building, even though for the last twenty-one years of its existence it was owned by an architectural firm and housed many and varied tenants.

2009 Some of the old schools are gone; miraculously, some remain. John H. Daniel School and the Brothers' School are gone but the George Washington School survives, as does the old Magruder School of my childhood.

    The aforementioned Woodrow Wilson Elementary School is long gone but the Walter Reed school building still survives.

| THE
BOYS'
SCHOOL

| AFTERWORD

Other schools were subsequently drawn. The Homer L. Ferguson High School was finally drawn in 2008.

When I learned that much of the building would be razed, with part of it to be incorporated into the Ferguson Center, designed by the renowned architect I. M. Pei, I visited the site.

I remember standing out in front of the school, mentally sketching it, and taking a photograph of it, wishing I had thought to do that of all those Peninsula buildings that were destroyed before I had a chance to sketch them on site.

Later, it was decided that the part of the high school left standing, but not seen in the drawing, would be razed.

Ferguson High School

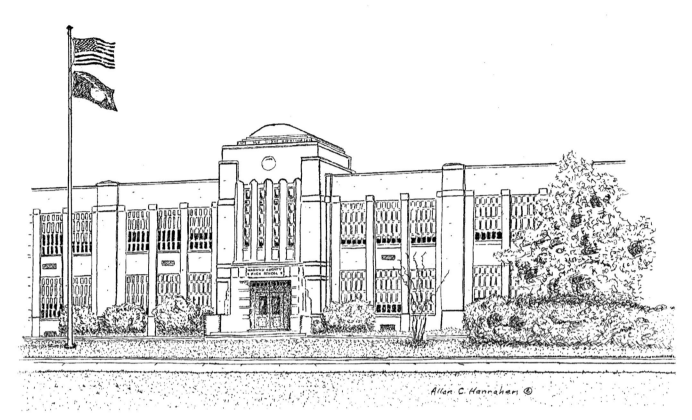

Warwick High School

October, 2009 After many years, my drawing of the front facade
of the old Warwick County High School, circa 1960, was finally
completed. Built in 1926 as Morrison High School, it became Warwick
County High School in 1948, and expanded to its present size in 1968
when the front facade portion was razed.

| AFTERWORD

Religion As Seen Through A Builder's Eyes

March 28, 1971

A church by any other name would be just as beautiful, when we consider its purpose on this earth. Whether it is a small, unpretentious structure serving a few loyal parishioners, or an imposing, massive edifice having members numbered in the thousands, a church has appeal because of its mission in the lives of men: worship of the deity; salvation of souls; moral uplifting of society; and generally the betterment of mankind.

Just as there are different beliefs and modes of worship in the realm of Christianity (which is the Religion presented here) there are different wants in the form and function of the physical church – the building – even within the same denomination.

Individual congregations may assume a great or nominal role in the design of the building but in any case they have the final say because after all, they are ones who have to pay for it. The chosen style, or form, is matched and merged with the function and a new "house of worship" is transformed from idea to paper to mortar, wood, brick, and glass.

In recent years some congregations have been more concerned

with use, or function, and the church, in its external appearance may resemble an office building or school. And though these particular churches still undertake the same laudable mission their aesthetic appeal is diminished because we tend to equate them with secular rather than totally with the ethereal.

In the accompanying drawings can be seen the chronological progression of architecture over the past two thousand years, although all of these churches were built in this century. However, just as there are many, many other beautiful churches on the Peninsula, so there are other styles of architecture but most are refinements or extensions of these drawn.

Strong and imposing is the Roman style of Saint Vincent de Paul Catholic Church at Thirty-third Street and Huntington Avenue. A

ST. VINCENT DE PAUL

group of about thirty worshipers, out of which was to grow the St. Vincent's Parish, began meeting in a private home on Washington Avenue as early as 1881. Constructed in 1916, the present church and parish house now look down on the grave (marked by the statue) of the Rev. Fr. David F. Coleman who served from 1912 to the time of his death in 1932. The present pastor is the Rev. Thomas J. Quinlan.

SECOND PRESBYTERIAN | In harmony with its surroundings is the Second Presbyterian Church on Menchville Road, in Newport News.

Of contemporary design, this building is the fourth home of the Second Presbyterian congregation – one of the former locations being in the East End section of the city where it was pastored by this writer's grandfather during the years 1911 to 1914.

As a body, the church began April 23, 1899, and is now pastored by the Rev. Robert D. Goshorn.

Second Presbyterian Church

FIRST BAPTIST | Toward the heavens Gothic churches seem to soar, reaching toward the deity that is their reason for being. First Baptist Church of Newport News, on Twenty-ninth Street between Washington and West Avenues, is built in the Gothic style of pink Maine granite and has reached upward for these almost-seventy years since the laying of the cornerstone in 1902. However, in 1906 it was destroyed by fire but a man named Warner Twyford (he was on the reportorial staff of local publications) wrote: "But churchmen are traditionally stouthearted, and so, undismayed, they set about restoration, which was accomplished within another year."

The pastor of First Baptist is the Rev. W. Guy Webb.

Our colonial heritage is typified in one of the best – and probably the largest – examples of Georgian architecture on the Peninsula (excluding the originals of course) is Liberty Baptist Church, located near the intersection of Big Bethel Road and Todds Lane, in Hampton. The new sanctuary, dedicated in 1966, towers above the former sanctuary which itself was constructed as recently as 1952, attesting to the phenomenal growth of this church that has made the transition from rural to suburban to urban.

As a body, the church began in April of 1900 and is now pastored by the Rev. Jesse H. King, Jr.

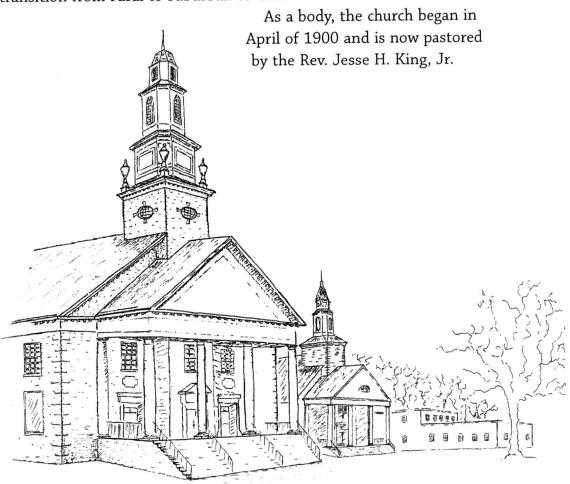

STS. CONSTANTINE AND HELEN GREEK ORTHODOX

The only one of its kind on the Peninsula is Saints Constantine and Helen Greek Orthodox Church located at Twenty-sixth and West Avenue. Of Byzantine style architecture, this church has served its congregation well these past twenty-odd years.

Weddings, funerals, confirmations, and other ceremonies of the church take place here, of course, but two events with which more local residents are becoming familiar are the annual bazaar held in the basement and the Epiphany service held in January.

It is then that the entire congregation proceeds to the C&O Pier 1 and the Priest, Peter H. Makris, blesses the waters, after which young men of the congregation dive for a wooden, gold-colored cross. It is a singular honor to whomever retrieves it.

2004 – 2011 Other than a turnover in pastors, Saint Vincent de Paul Catholic Church is still a viable entity in downtown Newport News. However, the Saint Vincent's High School, later named Peninsula Catholic, moved from the downtown section of the city to Harpersville Road.

Other than a change in pastors, the Second Presbyterian Church also remains in place, still a place of worship for its congregation.

After a transition period, First Baptist Church of Newport News made the move to midtown, next to the Peninsula Memorial Park cemetery on Warwick Boulevard. Their former building is now home to the Calvary Revival Church, Peninsula.

The Rev. Jesse H. King, Jr., pastor of Liberty Baptist Church, died in the pulpit on an Easter morning after completing his sermon. There have been a number of pastors since, and the church body has moved to a huge new plant at 1221 Big Bethel Road, about a quarter-mile away. Their former building is now home to the Warwick Assembly of God, which was formerly located in Newport News on Harpersville Road at Terrace Drive. That congregation was forced to relocate when their building had to give way to the new Hampton Roads Center Parkway.

The former Saints Constantine and Helen Greek Orthodox Church building now sits vacant. The new church building is located on Traverse Road off of J. Clyde Morris Boulevard, close to Interstate 64. The Rev. Makris has retired, and the Rev. George Chioros is the priest now.

In the ensuing years, attempts to render other churches have been made. First Presbyterian at 215 Thirty-second Street in downtown Newport News was drawn when it was still a viable house of worship under that name. Sadly, though, First Presbyterian Church saw a steady decrease in its congregation, and no longer exists. The building is now home to the Full Gospel Kingdom Church.

The Warwick Assembly of God on Harpersville Road was sketched in the Eighties when it was still standing. The building was razed in the late nineties to help make way for the continuation of the Hampton Roads Center Parkway into Newport News. A "green space" at the northeast corner of the intersection of Harpersville Road, Hampton Roads Center Parkway, and Terrace Drive now marks roughly where the building once stood. The church congregation took up new residence in the former home of Liberty Baptist Church at 1228 Todd's Lane, Hampton, Virginia, but moved again in 2010.

A small, stylized drawing of Trinity Methodist Church in downtown Newport News was done years ago, and a while back, in response to a patron's request, was redrawn to reflect more of that lovely building's interesting details.

Other Peninsula churches sketched (but not included in this collection) over the years include: Newmarket Baptist, next to the former Newmarket North Shopping Mall; Saint Rose of Lima Catholic Church in the Wythe section of Hampton; Saint Joan of Arc Catholic Church on George Washington Highway (Route 17) in York County; Saint Andrews Episcopal Church in Hilton Village in Newport News; and First (Black) Baptist Church on Jefferson Avenue in Newport News. Perhaps those drawings will find a home in a later book.

Trinity Methodist Church

It All Started Here!

November 21, 1971

Berkeley, patented in 1618, is probably the most visited and historic of the plantations that sit majestic along the James. Here, in 1619, was held the first Thanksgiving in the New World, a fact that is slowly, but most certainly becoming known.

The mansion was constructed over a century after the event – in 1726 – but for the past two hundred and forty-odd years has presided serenely over this land that once felt the weight of those men of long-ago days who gathered here to celebrate and give thanks for that which The Almighty had bestowed upon them.

Therefore, let us give thanks, silently or otherwise, for what we have, and may we preserve and cherish it so that two hundred and forty-odd years from now men will think kindly of us men of "long-ago-days."

Oh yes, a few years after the First Thanksgiving at Berkeley a similar event took place in the New England colony of Massachusetts.

Berkeley still thrives and survives as a destination for history-loving tourists.

Inexplicably, a lot of America still believes that the first Thanksgiving was celebrated in New England, so the campaign to educate them otherwise continues apace.

Berkeley

Old Mills Are Relics Of The Past

April 2, 1972

CAUSEY'S
MILL

In this age of store-bought bread, packaged flour and other such over-processed grain products of automated, assembly-line factories, the local mill evokes the same contrast as would the spinning wheel if that quaint device were compared to the modern thread and yarn factory. However, as archaic and bucolic a structure as the old mills are in this age, three of them still exist on the Peninsula, and one of these is in working condition with finished product for sale. Stranger still, it appears as though all three will stand for some years to come, thanks to the efforts of concerned individuals and groups as well as just plain circumstance.

Traveling north on Warwick Boulevard you first come upon Causey's Mill, located on the shore of Lake Maury, also called Museum Lake, and in former years known as Water's Creek. This mill is identified by a signboard – seen from Warwick Blvd. – that gives its date as 1866, the year that Mr. Causey bought and restored it to working condition. But it is said to have been built originally before 1681 (when it was owned by a Capt. John Langthorne) with a few of the original timbers still in the structure.

Few records exist that give the mill's ownership or history over the years but during the Revolutionary War, Virginia Volunteers under a Captain Edward Mallory clashed at Water's Creek with a British force of forty men on a foraging expedition. The British officer was killed, his men routed and forced to retreat. Local legend has it that the millpond dam (which was on the opposite side of the mill from the highway) is where the skirmish took place.

A man named Smith is supposed to have owned the mill during the War Between The States, when it was considerably damaged, and then Mr. Causey bought it.

Causey's Mill – *Hard by Warwick Blvd., on the shore of Lake Maury, the waters of which are seen to the side of and behind the mill in this view, looking south.*

In 1890 the Newport News Water Company purchased the mill as well as the mill pond and property around it but the mill is reported to have still been in operation even in to the Twentieth Century. However, the mill was eventually abandoned and fell in to disrepair prior to 1930, when The Mariners' Museum purchased so much of the property in the area. At that time The Mariners' Museum restored the mill to its appearance of an earlier era.

YOUNG'S MILL | Continuing northwest on Warwick Boulevard for approximately four miles brings you to Young's Mill, designated by a Historical marker that begins, "Since early colonial days Deep Creek has had a dam and

*Young's Mill –
Looking north,
shows a side of the
mill opposite from
that which will be
seen by motorists
traveling the new
section of Warwick
Blvd. between Deep
Creek Road and
Menchville Road.*

pond here with a mill, owned by the Mathews, Digges, and Young Families, grinding corn well into the 20th Century. In the Peninsular Campaign, Federal forces of Gen. McClellan encountered strong Confederate works nearby, the right flank of Gen. Magruder's first line of defense."

The Federals were unsuccessful in breaching the Confederate lines because the Historical marker concludes, "The works were abandoned April 5, 1862, (this was almost six months later) for a resolute stand six miles farther at Lee's Mill."

Young's Mill was spared during McClellan's invasion but a little more than a hundred years later, in 1964, another invading force swept by, this one known as the Virginia Highway Department, and the mill seemed doomed to certain destruction. Fortunately, their line of march (the new route of this stretch of Warwick Blvd.) was turned aside enough to insure the mill's survival.

ROBERTSON'S WINDMILL

Leaving Young's Mill and continuing north and west for approximately eighteen miles you reach Colonial Williamsburg and Robertson's Windmill. This post-type mill consists of a main structure, called the house, which is balanced on a large center post and rotated by means of a large pole and wagon wheel so that the mill is kept facing into the wind. With a wind of ten or fifteen miles per hour, approximately three pounds of corn meal can be ground per minute and this meal can be purchased at the mill.

Post mills of this type were numerous throughout Virginia and were usually located close to a town or city although such plantations as Gov. Yeardley's Flowerdew Hundred Plantation, south of the James river, included a windmill on the property.

Many mills have existed on the Peninsula in bygone years, such as the one that gave the name "Tide Mill," to a section of Hampton and

Robertson's Windmill
– Located on North England Street in Colonial Williamsburg. This post-type mill has been reconstructed on the site where it stood in 1721.

the windmill that was on the grounds of the historic Herbert House in Hampton. But as the need for them decreased, naturally so did their number. It is fortunate that these three examples exist so we may at least know what they looked like.

AFTERWORD | ***2004*** Causey's Mill has, this year, again come to the fore. It has been reported that as recently as March of this year there has been work underway to help preserve this "relic of the past," through a partnership of the Mariners Museum, the Riverside Regional Medical Center (Hospital), and the city of Newport News. In addition to preservation work on the mill itself, an access road and a little park around the mill are planned.

Young's Mill, in the Nineties, took a direct hit from one of its nearby trees, which partially destroyed the structure. The city of Newport News restored the old mill to its prior appearance.

Robertson's Windmill, maintained assiduously by Colonial Williamsburg, remains as it was, with one addition. A colonial-style, split-rail fence now encircles the site so that casual passersby cannot just wander up for a look, which is understandable. After building it, Colonial Williamsburg now maintains and "interprets" it, and that does not come cheap.

2006 Causey's Mill still has not been restored. The project has taken longer than expected, partly because bids for the work came in well over expectations, but it is expected that revised requests for bids for foundation work will be issued in September and, hopefully, work will begin in mid-fall. After that foundation work is done the city museums' carpenters will go to work on the roof and exterior walls.

July, 2009 Causey's Mill, while supposedly restored, is at present in dire need of a coat of paint.

October, 2010   A lovely hillside park now overlooks Causey's Mill and Lake Maury.

February, 2011   A recent visit to Causey's Mill revealed a deteriorating foundation and other signs of aging not addressed.

2012   Thankfully, Causey's Mill is moved about 20 feet west, placed on a new foundation, and restored.

Lest We Forget... Those Who Sleep

May 24, 1970

VICTORY ARCH | Beneath the wooden predecessor of this Arch marched returning warriors of World War I, accorded "Greetings With Love," while their fallen comrades slept amid a "Triumph With Tears."

And now an eternal flame burns in memoriam to all those who have fallen in this country's service. How fitting it is that this Arch and this Flame should be situated here, for from here the "callow youth" departed and to here the surviving men returned.

And let us recall that a Virginia lady, Cassandra Oliver Moncure, is credited with setting aside May 30 as a day to honor (originally) the dead of both the North and the South during the War Between The States – a war that saw so many battles fought, and so much blood shed, on this Virginia soil.

Now, on Memorial Day, we honor the dead of all wars in which this nation has struggled. Let us pray that the list of wars grows no longer.

Newport News Victory Arch

Now They Dream Of God And Country

HAMPTON NATIONAL CEMETERY MONUMENT

May 27, 1973

Silent stands the sentinel in granite strength as it casts its shadow across this final resting place of so many brave servants of our Republic. Sixty-five feet the obelisk reaches upwards above this "bivouac of the dead" known as the Hampton National Cemetery. And on the base of the monument is the inscription, "In Memory Of Union Soldiers Who Died To Maintain The Laws."

But look close at the headstone telling that this ground also holds the final remains of opponents of that union: those who felt their allegiance was to a Cause, or to their home state against other states.

And just as Memorial Day began during the War Between The States, so did this cemetery. The Day and this Ground have come down through more than a century together until this Memorial Day when we honor the dead of all wars in which this Nation has engaged, and of which survivors and victims alike are interred here.

Make no mistake, war is accorded no honor here; no, but the brave souls who were asked by their country to go to war – and were claimed by that war – are so honored here.

AFTERWORD | *2009* All that seems to have changed here is that there are now more residents. One of them is a beloved older sister of this writer.

The wife of a veteran of the U.S. Army, Naomi Hanrahan Kammerzell was a cancer victim, dying in 1989 at the age of 58. She now rests a stone's throw from the monument.

Her husband, former Staff Sergeant Irvin George Kammerzell, dying in September, 2009, has joined her in rest.

Hampton National Cemetery

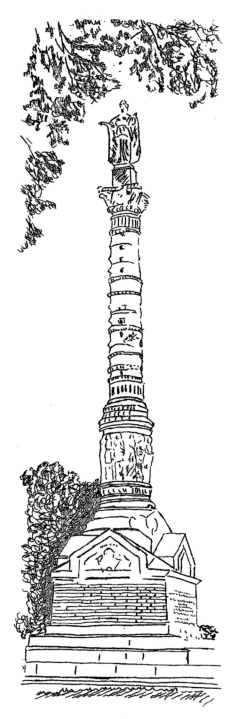

"Lines Composed At Yorktown"

The yellow plastic rope snakes its way down Moore House Road
And sets apart the sun-spattered crowds
That stand and loll and stroll the Battlefield:
Ground hallowed by those of freedom's struggle.
But behind a shield transparent the oratory –
Words of freedom from behind a see-through shield.

In review the troops file past,
Then rank-on-rank of grey step down the road –
    Virginia's own,
And a rainbow follows on:
Colors dazzling in October's sun,
Uniforms two-centuries-old clothe hundreds and hundreds,
Shoulder-to-shoulder in measured pace down
    Moore House Road;
Sunlight flashing from bayonets,
Marching music stirring the smiling throngs,
Sought the likes of which we'll never see again.

Yorktown Monument

South-by-east a stack in silhouette
Pokes its snout above the tree line, breathing darkly,
And helicopters hang above the tree tops:
Hear them: hwhup, hwhup, hwhup.
Trailing tendrils of colored mist, eagles soar down
The cloud-spotted sky and step to earth and hands clap, clap, clap.

Ranks form on the "surrender field,"
Moved to here for convenience sake;
Flags furled, weapons grounded,
and fifes and drums send music forth:
"The World Turned Upside Down,"
Echoed by cannons' booming salute.
Buses await so we turn and walk away,
Recalling sights the likes of which we'll never see again.

October 1981
A.C.H.

Out of the Rubble...

November 19, 1972

HAMPTON | The price of progress is seldom picayunish, and the progress transpiring in downtown Hampton – known in recent years as Old Hampton – is not without its price as witnessed by the disappearance of old homes and business buildings, the likes of which "shall not pass this way again." Falling under the assault of the wrecking crane and the bulldozer, these demolished buildings will be replaced by a pedestrian mall or, ironically, older-looking structures than those demolished because as most everyone knows by now, Old Hampton is to be decidedly and authentically colonial in appearance – a very pleasant prospect.

Rising from the rubble is not a new experience for Hampton, sometimes referred to in the past as the "Gamecock Town." Thrice before, this "oldest continuous English-speaking settlement in America" has had to turn to the task of reconstruction. During the War of Independence, on October 24, 1775, British forces cannoned the town starting several fires; one of which was at the parish church, St. John's. Four score and six years later, in August, 1861, Confederate soldiers, many of whom were natives of the community, put the torch to the town to prevent its use by the Union. More than one hundred and thirty homes and stores were destroyed in the ensuing conflagration. Then in April of 1884 another catastrophic fire swept the area – down both sides of Queen Street – and destroyed a total of thirty-three buildings. Some of the buildings that were demolished this past Spring were products of the reconstruction that took place in the aftermath of that fire. *For example:*

Woodward's Pharmacy was built in 1885 on the northwest corner of the intersection of King and Queen Streets. This landmark – probably the finest example of Victorian architecture in the city –

Woodward's Pharmacy

Merchants National Bank was originally the First National Bank of Hampton. It became the Woodward Pharmacy in September, 1934 (the bank failed to reopen after the Bank Holiday in 1933) and during a part of its career as a pharmacy it also served as the Greyhound Bus Terminal. It was razed during the last days of March, 1972.

The **Merchants National Bank** building on the northeast corner of the intersection of King and Queen Streets was relatively new, dating only since 1920. It was razed during March, 1972. The Merchants

National Bank, founded in 1903, became the Virginia National Bank in 1965 and is now located in the new, colonial-style building on the southeast corner of the intersection of King and Queen Streets.

North King Street. This row of buildings on the west side of North King Street was located north of Woodward's Pharmacy and demolished about the same time as Woodward's. The buildings took in the addresses number Nine to Number Twenty-seven North King Street and Langley Cabs was one of the better-known tenants.

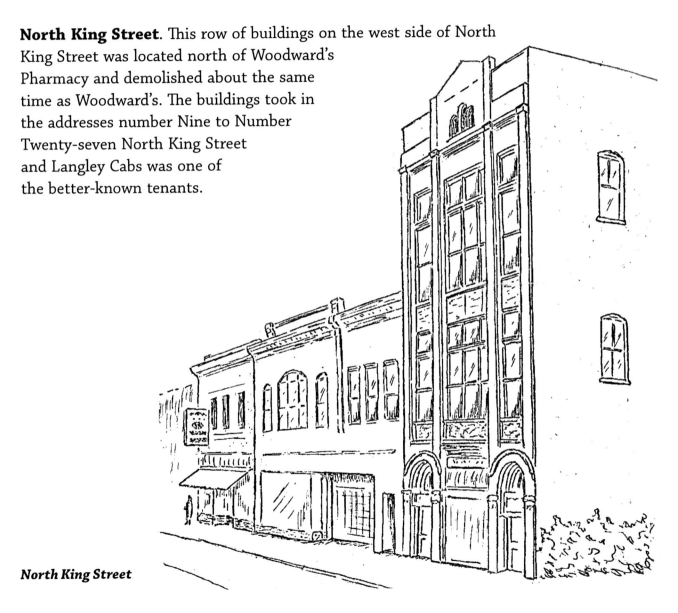

North King Street

2013 The **Citizens and Marine Bank** building, built in 1900, was the home of the Bank of Hampton, established in 1881. Reputedly the largest bank in the city, the Bank of Hampton, along with the First National Bank of Hampton, closed in April of 1933 due to the financial situation at that time, and re-opened that summer as the Citizens National Bank. In the sixties, it merged with Citizens and Marine Bank in Newport News, which was soon taken over by United

Citizens and Marine Bank

Virginia Bank. This building was demolished in the spring of 1975. Note: Probably due to space constraints, this drawing, along with the caption, was not a part of the originally published article.

South King Street. This building is about the last of the nineteenth-century buildings on South King Street and housed many business concerns over the years. Still standing as this is written, the building will probably be destroyed sometime this Fall or Winter.

A block or so distant from the commercial area is that residential section of Hampton that was first settled during Colonial times and is known as **Pee Dee**. The origination of the name lies buried and unknown somewhere in the past. The area is now considered to be that land bounded by Settlers Landing Road on the west, the Hampton River on the east, a cove of the River on the north and Cary Street on the south. The strip of land along Cary Street was once known as Mill Point, owing to the fact that a windmill once stood on the point, and four of the five stately nineteenth-century homes that stood there were destroyed as

South King Street

of August 10, 1972. The first house on the left (in the drawing) is still standing and still being used by the Hampton School Administration.

At the time this is written Pee Dee is one of the areas under consideration as a site for the new Hampton City Hall that will replace the present one built in 1938 on North King Street. In addition to the controversy over location there is also the controversy accompanying the proposed modern design of the new municipal center, with some wondering how compatible the proposed modern design will be with Old Hampton when the "renewal" of the commercial area reaches completion.

In any case, let it be murmured that, hopefully, Old Hampton

**Pee Dee
Point**

will be nurtured and maintained: allowed to truly grow "olde" before another "urban renewal" takes place.

2006 The building on South King Street, like the others chronicled, was indeed demolished.

The new city hall was constructed, but obviously not on Pee Dee; a cluster of condominiums now occupy that area, and the first house on the left is now gone, as well.

While on the subject of Pee Dee, the drawing of it was done from the old Hampton River bridge, to the occasional shout from people in autos crossing over it. That bridge is gone now, replaced by another one that is more aligned with Settlers Landing Road.

They're Tearing The Town Down!

September 17, 1970

NEWPORT
NEWS

Like some primeval predator, the bulldozer snarls and growls and points its steel, square snout at the object of the past and, aided by the wrecking ball swung like the proboscis of some prehistoric mastodon, transforms that object into a memory, to the accompaniment of a cacophony: *BLAM! POW! BANG! CRA-A-A-SH!*

Now, there is room for a dream of the future: a dream that will replace these views of downtown Newport News that have been – or soon will be – demolished, necessary sacrifices to the municipal surgery taking place.

Phoenix-like, a new "downtown" is rising from the rubble of the old – the old that was tasteless and ugly, and the old that was charming and pleasant to look upon.

Someone – a preacher to be exact – once said, "Appreciate the past, yes, but do not worship the past." He could have added, "Grieve for the past, yes, but be glad of the future."

Our hopes, though, are that the future "downtown" will be beneficial – directly or otherwise – to most everyone; that it has a longer life than did the past, and that good does not have to co-exist with bad. Redevelopment is worth the price if our hopes are realized; if they are not . . . .

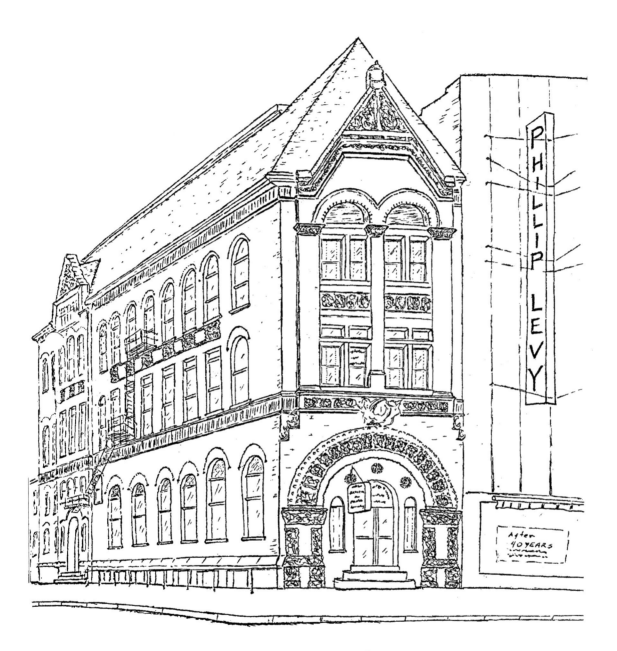

The old **Citizens and Marine Bank Building** at 2701 Washington Avenue is another downtown landmark that is due to fall before the bulldozer.

*These former rooming houses on **West Avenue** have been demolished in the name of redevelopment. On the left is the well-remembered West Avenue Tearoom.*

*This row of buildings on lower **Washington Avenue** is among the last due to come down. The city's newest downtown building, the First and Merchants' "skyscraper" can be seen in the upper left background.*

AFTERWORD | *2006* Yes, they all came down. And some, but not all, would be replaced, as a later piece will show.

A sketch from that period is added here. It is a downtown street scene, the two-hundred block of Twenty-seventh Street, to be exact. The Salvation Army was located there at the time.

*Near **Washington Avenue***

AN ODE TO NEWPORT NEWS

A Sweet-Town Building

December 1, 1974

SONGS AND
POEMS OF
NEWPORT
NEWS

Newport News is home sweet home to most of its approximately one-hundred-and-fifty-thousand population and it borders "the roadstead well known to all maritime circles," according to Collis P. Huntington (1821-1900). But Newport News is not Paris, or London, or San Francisco, or even a smaller version of any of these, thus it is unlikely it will ever have a Top-Ten tune written about it. This probability hardly poses a disgrace, however, especially when we consider Los Angeles's dozen futile years of competition for an official song to match the appeal of "I Left My Heart in San Francisco," the theme song of its rival city to the north.

The foregoing is not meant to imply that Newport News has failed altogether to be recognized in words and music because this city that hugs the River James has already been immortalized in at least two poems and two songs. Henry Wadsworth Longfellow (1807-1882), that giant of American literature, was author of one of those poems ("A Nameless Grave"), which follows on page 63.

Ninety years or so after Joaquin Miller called it "a sweet-town building," Newport News is building again, as seen looking across the "super-block" acreage from West Avenue. To the left is the First & Merchants National Bank building, completed in the Spring of 1969; in the center is a construction crane being used in building the new police headquarters and jail; to the right is the United Virginia Bank building, scheduled for completion in December, 1974; and beyond that is City Hall, completed in the early Spring of '72.

"A Nameless Grave"

"A soldier of the Union mustered out"
Is the inscription on an unknown grave
At Newport News, beside the salt-sea wave,
Nameless and dateless, sentinel or scout
Show down in skirmish, or disastrous rout
Of battle when the loud artillery drave
Its iron wedges through the ranks of brave
And doomed battalions, storming the redoubt.
Thou unknown here sleeping by the sea
In the forgotten grave! With secret shame
I feel my pulses beat, my forehead burn,
When I remember thou hadst given for
All that thou hadst, thy life, thy very name,
And I can give thee nothing in return.

Joaquin Miller (1837-1913), called the "Poet of the Sierras," because of his affection for that area of the country of which he wrote and in which he lived, wrote the following poem in the 1880s while visiting Newport News as the guest of Collis P. Huntington, the founder of the Newport News Shipbuilding and Dry Dock Company. Actually named Cincinnatus Hiner Miller, he took the name of Joaquin (pronounced *wah KEEN*) after the name of the Mexican bandit, Joaquin Murietta, whom Miller had once defended in an article.

"Newport News"

The huge sea monster, the "Merrimac";
The mad sea monster, the "Monitor";
You may sweep the sea, peer forward and back,
But never a sign or a sound of war.
A vulture or two in the heavens blue;
A sweet town building, a boatman's call;
The far sea-song of a pleasure crew;
The sound of hammers. And that is all.
And where are the monsters that tore this main?
And where are the monsters that shook this shore?
The sea crew mad! And the shore shot flame!
The mad sea monsters they are no more.
The palm, and the pine, and the sea sands brown;
The far sea songs of the pleasure crews;
The air like balm in this building town—
And that is the picture of Newport News.

It is an interesting coincidence that the epic encounter that ushered in the age of iron ships transpired offshore of where a city was to grow to fame and fortune with the building of **iron ships**.

The songs and poems of Newport News all allude to the sea, and ships and the men who sail them. At the south end of the **Shipyard** is the Chester W. Nimitz, *a nuclear carrier scheduled for commissioning in the late Summer or early Autumn of 1975.*

"The Nameless Grave" and "Newport News" are both inscribed on mounted tablets located close by the statue of Collis P. Huntington in Christopher Newport Park in downtown Newport News. The park, bounded by Twenty-eighth Street, the Newport Towers Apartments and the Greyhound Bus Station and Twenty-sixth Street, looks out over the James River.

Newport News is a city of the present, as well as the past, as evidenced by two contemporary songs. One of the songs is entitled: "Was a Sunny Day" and was written by Paul Simon and copyrighted in 1973. Paul Simon, as many are aware, was also the author of such hits as "Bridge Over Troubled Waters," "Mrs. Robinson," and "Sounds of Silence" – the latter two being part of the sound track of the motion picture, "The Graduate."

"Was a Sunny Day" describes a particular day while telling about a sailor who was stationed "in Newport News," and his girl friend, Lorelei, who was a high school queen who called him "Speedoo," although his name was Mr. Earl.

In the accompanying drawing that shows the Carrier *Nimitz*, there was once a tree-shaded slope to the right, near where the automobile parking deck is now. And some time around a quarter-century ago this writer, still a youngster, observed a young sailor and his companion, a young and beautiful red-haired lady. He was in a crisp, white uniform and she was in a billowy, summer dress and they sat on that slope, spending part of what "was a sunny day." Mr. Earl and Lorelei? Who knows?

Another contemporary song mentioning Newport News was written by two Virginia gentlemen, Don and Harold Reid, one half of the award-winning Statler Brothers group (the other members are Lew DeWitt and Phil Balsley). Although they hail from Staunton, Virginia, the members of the group have performed all over the country, as well as abroad, and for more than eight years they toured with Johnny Cash. They now entertain – as a group – more or less autonomously and are described as "the entertainers on and off record."

The Statler Brothers have produced at least five albums and their brand of music, usually classed as country, falls in that area where country music and popular music overlap and blend. And the themes are usually of an everyday nature, as illustrated by the song, "A Special Song for Wanda," copyrighted in 1972 and quoted here by permission of the authors.

"A Special Song for Wanda"

Wanda was alone at nights while he was somewhere sailin'
A navy wife with too much spare time on her hands.
His letters were a comfort and I think she really loved him,
But paper words don't fill the space when someone needs a man.
And I'd just like to sing a special song for Wanda,
'Cause Wanda was a special friend of mine.
And somewhere, makin' up his bed in Newport News, Virginia,
I hope Wanda hears my song and plays it one more time.

Wanda gave me ev'rything a body ever needed
But a body's needs will sometimes lead a soul to sin.
She was only lonesome, a wife on leave of duty;
She went down in history and prob'ly will again.
And I'd just like to sing a special song for Wanda,
'Cause Wanda was a special friend of mine.
And somewhere makin' up his bed in Newport News, Virginia
I hope Wanda hears my song and plays it one more time.

So Newport News is not without its publicists who have written works that touch on the City and reflect feelings about it that range from the very human and commonplace to the epochal and sublime.

AFTERWORD | ***2006*** Some years after the above article was written, my wife Renee and I were in a bookstore in Hilton Village that specialized in old books and other such antique works. As I recall, the store was owned by the retired minister of Riverside Baptist Church, the Rev. Hamilton, and operated by his son. Anyhow, Renee called my attention to a sheaf of sheet music. I picked it up, looked at it, and immediately bought it.

With words written in 1918 by Sergeant Hal Oliver, music by Corporal Willie Shifrin, "sung with great success by Frederick V. Bowers," and "Dedicated to our Commanding Officer Col. E. P. Orton," it was . . .

"Newport News Blues"

I've been around the world a bit, I've seen 'bout all the sights –
I've heard a lot of melodies about the gay white lights.
But when I went to Newport News I heard real southern blues,
The blues is all that you can hear down there in Newport News

Chorus:
Oh! Newport News Blues is the latest fad,
Newport News Blues will surely drive you mad,
You start in to jazz, then you raz-ma-taz,
Oh, way down south in the land of cotton
Your Uncle Sam has not forgotten,
You're away – a way far away from Broadway –
Newport News Blues is the fad down there,
They sing and dance that haunting melody –
Oh! when you're down in Newport News,
What do they want to play that doggone blues for?
The blues of Newport News.

I've traveled here, I've traveled there, from darkness to white lights
But now I wish that I were back among the southern nights.
For when I hear those darkies' voices chant that draggy blues,
I tell you folks I wish I were again in Newport News.

(Repeat chorus)

AFTERWORD | *Re* the drawings of downtown, the First & Merchants National Bank was merged into NationsBank, which has since been merged into Bank of America and well may yet be merged into some other bank. The United Virginia Bank has been merged into Crestar Bank, and the jail and police department have been joined by a new courthouse that fronts Washington Avenue between Twenty-fifth and

Twenty-sixth streets. A new police department building has been constructed on the north side of Jefferson Avenue between Mercury Boulevard and Main Street.

The *Monitor* and the *Virginia* (*Merrimac*) fought their momentous battle, and now a battle is underway at The Mariners' Museum to preserve the turret of the *Monitor*, retrieved from the ocean bottom.

*The construction of the north-side addition to the **Shipyard** – as viewed from River Road near Seventy-third Street – is depicted in this sketch of October fourteenth. Although work on the first ship is expected to begin around the middle of 1975, it will be six months later before the site construction is completed.*

Frail Ghosts Of A Bygone Era

November 14, 1971

Eight or more times daily a metal behemoth lumbers the length of the Peninsula and no one makes any attempt to stop it! In fact, some people even wish it would travel its unimpeded way more often; and strangely enough, the Federal Government is subsidizing some of its Peninsular prowls.

Of course we're referring to the trains of the Chesapeake and Ohio Railway Company, and the much-in-the-news Amtrak system of inter-city passenger trains. That is today.

Let's go back into yesterday – ninety years to the beginning: there in the Autumn of 1881, at a point somewhere along the three-and-a-half-mile stretch of C & O Railway roadbed between the old Colonial capital of Williamsburg and the crossroads of Ewell, a maul cleaved the air and inscribed an arc as it was brought down upon the head of a silver spike, again and again until the spike could be driven no farther into the burnt umber-colored cross-tie.

The maul wielder (Major J. J. Gordon) stepped back from his toil, wiped the dew of labor from his forehead and acknowledged the cheers of those in attendance. Now, Richmond and points west on the C & O line were tied to the sea at a sleepy hamlet named Newport News.

Collis P. Huntington, one of the great railroad builders of the latter Nineteenth Century, had once again laid his tracks in pursuit of his grand plan, which was to have a track from coast to coast under one railroad administration.

It would be May of 1882 before the roadbed would be stable enough to allow trains to travel the entire distance between Richmond and Newport News, but trains did carry passengers en route to Yorktown to the Centennial celebration of Cornwallis' Surrender. An old newspaper described the trip as follows: "The grandest pageant of

Lee Hall station was built in the early 1900's. The far section was added in the early 1930's. At one time the stationmaster lived on the second floor. It still serves as a freight station.

all from the foundation of the Commonwealth occurred about dark on October 19, 1881, when old Williamsburg witnessed six passenger trains filled with troops pass through en route to Yorktown."

In 1882, was finished an extension from Newport News to Old Point Comfort by way of Hampton and Phoebus. Now, travelers could more easily reach that seashore resort, the old Hygeia Hotel.

There were no depots or freight stations to speak of those first few years but they were not long in coming. Let's call the roll of those not shown, the ones that have come and gone.

The Toano station, demolished in November 1967, leaves behind only the thoroughfare on which it stood, Depot Street.

The Oriana station, built in 1942, is officially listed as still standing but this writer could find no traces of the structure still standing above ground.

On the extension of track to Old Point was constructed two depots – one in Hampton on Washington Street and the other in Phoebus close to Mallory Street. The former was built In 1891, added to in 1917 and 1940, and demolished in September, 1970. The latter was probably built around the same time and reportedly destroyed by fire eight or nine years ago.

So there it is, the C & O down the Peninsula – ninety years old and changing.

The End Of The Line station still stands, but presently serves as The Train Station restaurant. The shed over the tracks is now gone, as are the tracks themselves.

End of the Line: *That applies to the tracks at the Newport News station because 200 feet farther the tracks change from steel to water and the roadbed becomes the silt of the James River bottom. This station was built in 1940. The first station was built in 1902 and later demolished. Under Amtrak, Newport News still serves passengers.*

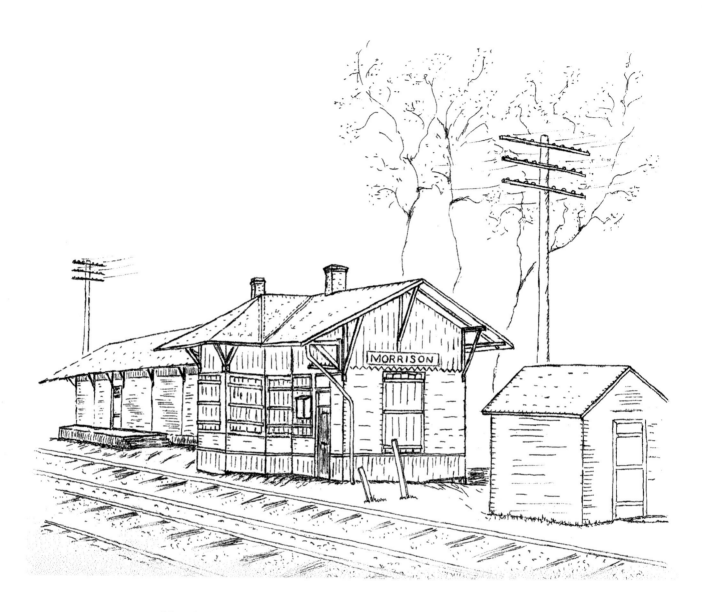

Morrison *station was razed May 13, 1971, less than two weeks after this drawing was made. The windows were boarded even then.*

Oyster Point station was built in 1942, relocated at the present site in 1946. It was entirely removed less than a month ago.

The **Reservoir** shelter, decaying quietly, rests now beside the C & O tracks at this no-longer-used whistle loop.

The **Williamsburg** station was built in 1935 in keeping with the Restoration.
This station stills serves passengers as well as freight.

2006-2009   The Lee Hall station underwent a "sprucing up" in 1981 in observance of the bicentennial of the British surrender at Yorktown in 1781. The past twenty-three years have taken their toll, but the station still stands, even though unused. There are plans underfoot to move it for traffic reasons.

The Williamsburg station essentially remains as is, and continues to serve Amtrak riders.

The Reservoir shelter could not be located, so it is assumed that it has decayed away.

The Oyster Point station was moved to the Blue Bird Gap Farm in Hampton.

2009   Over three days, June 23-25, the Lee Hall Station was moved to the other side of the tracks, and will become a museum.

The "End of the Line" is today located a few miles up the tracks, and across Warwick Boulevard from the old steam locomotive that is permanently on display in Huntington Park. In observance of the aforementioned bicentennial of the surrender at Yorktown, a new Amtrak station was built here and aptly named "Lafayette Square."

Lafayette

An historical marker was erected and reads as follows:

Lafayette Square

Dedicated October 1981 as a Bicentennial Observance in Honor of the MARQUIS DE LAFAYETTE, 1757 – 1834, Washington's Beloved "Boy General". The Young Frenchman's Extraordinary Devotion To the Cause of American Independence And His Skill in the Martial Arts Contributed Largely to the Signal Victory at the Battle Of Yorktown, Insuring the Independence of the American Colonies and Forever Endearing Him To His Adopted America.

Newport News Historical Committee, 1981

Peninsula Newspaper Buildings, Past And Present

October 1, 1972

Recently, President Nixon publicly proclaimed the week beginning Sunday, October eighth as National Newspaper Week; therefore, what more appropriate time than this to recognize the local newspapers – both daily and weekly – that are serving the people of the Peninsula?

But first, what is a newspaper – that is, besides the obvious paper and ink?

In the material sense it must be realized that newspaper is first of all a business, and hopefully a money-making one. After all, if a newspaper loses money it either merges with another newspaper or it goes out of business; in either case that is a loss for the community as well as the employees and stockholders. A newspaper is a business that produces a product and in that product of paper and ink is contained the service of journalism: to inform, educate and entertain its customers as objectively (editorial page excluded), accurately and completely as possible while striving to remain within the popularly accepted bounds of good taste.

The original **Virginia Gazette** – Located on Duke of Gloucester St., the Printing Office and Post Office is where William Parks published the first Gazette. Partially destroyed by fire, the building has been restored to its original 1736 appearance.

The service performed by a newspaper business is accompanied by a great responsibility, and that responsibility is . . . the truth; not necessarily the absolute or real truth (because that is a Divine property), but the truth as best as can be determined by men and women reporting as accurately as possible what their senses, as well as other human beings, convey to them. Consequently, a newspaper conveys to its customers the day-to-day history that is taking place around them and mirrors an image, hopefully undistorted, of the fashion, style and culture of life as it exists.

Unfortunately, not all newspapers grow and prosper in their endeavors as witnessed by the August 31 shutdown of the *Newark (N.J.) Evening News*, the recent merger of the *Boston Herald-Traveler* with the *Boston Record American*, and the July 13 merger of the failing *Washington* (D.C.) *Daily News* with the Washington *Evening Star* – an event that prompted the publisher of the rival *Washington Post* to say the loss of any newspaper "is a loss to us all," speaking of those in the newspaper business. Hopefully, a long life will be enjoyed by all of the following local newspapers.

The Virginia Gazette. Established by William Parks in Williamsburg, Virginia on August 6, 1736, this was the first newspaper to be published in the Virginia Colony. There have been many "Gazettes" since 1736 but this revived weekly version has been in existence since 1930, commensurate with the Williamsburg Restoration, and carries the masthead set up by its first editor and publisher, William Parks, together with similar front-page format," according to Marian Osborne, a member of the *Gazette* staff who compiled a "Brief History" of the publication.

The Virginia Gazette – *Located on Prince George St., Williamsburg, for approximately 40 years, the Gazette moved this past August to this building on Second St. at Broadway.*

The Hampton Monitor. This newly revived weekly was originally established in 1836 but until August 8, 1972 had not been published since 1918. Coincidentally, it is printed by the Virginia Gazette.

The Daily Press and The Times-Herald. The *Daily Press* morning daily was founded on January 4, 1896. In March, 1913, it was merged with the *Times-Herald*, an evening daily which itself had been formed out of a merger on December 26, 1901.

So, as we enjoy the local newspapers' practicing, it seems, an unspoken fealty to the "public's right to know," let us be reminded to thank the First Amendment to the United States Constitution that guarantees their freedom: "Congress shall make no law . . . abridging the freedom of speech; or of the press . . . ."

About the time the article was published, my eldest son, Gary, became a carrier for the *Daily Press* and *Times-Herald*. A few years later, my younger son, Gregory, became a carrier also.

Hampton Monitor

Daily Press and Times-Herald – *This was the newspaper's home in downtown Newport News for 58 years, dating back to 1910. The building passed to the Redevelopment and Housing Commission and has since been demolished.*

Daily Press and Times-Herald – *This building of classic contemporary design was completed in 1968.*

AFTERWORD | **2006**   The new Daily Press and Times-Herald plant has been added on to over the years but the main building has not been altered noticeably. The newspaper was purchased by *The Chicago Tribune*. The *Times-Herald* ceased publication.

The *Virginia Gazette* was purchased by the Daily Press, Inc. in the nineties, and moved into a new building at 216 Ironbound Road.

The *Hampton Monitor* lasted only a few years.

2008   In July of that year the decision was made to do a drawing of the "new" *Virginia Gazette* building on Ironbound Road.

The Virginia Gazette

2012 In July the presses of the *Daily Press* were silenced and the newspaper was outsourced to a printer in Hanover County, north of Richmond. In late August of that same year the *Daily Press* campus was put on the market.

2013 In early February we stopped by the Daily Press to buy a back issue. A man and a woman were out front of the building putting up banners that proclaimed, "We're Moving!" The banners stated that the move would take place in 2013. Those banners, along with the "For Sale" sign, made for a sad scene.

How To Speak Charlestonese Like A Charlestonian

March 22, 1970

CHARLESTON,
SOUTH
CAROLINA

EDITOR'S NOTE: The author, a Peninsula resident, seems to have a special "feeling" for Charleston, S.C. as evidenced by his articles on the King's English, as it is spoken with a Charlestonese dialect, and the pen sketches that he made of some of its charming pre-Civil War landmarks during a recent visit.

Imagine yourself: you're strolling down the sidewalk alongside the Battery, or "Bottry" as a Charlestonian would pronounce the name of that historic section of his city. Shaded by the Spanish moss and magnolia – and palmetto – you gaze idly out across the harbor toward Fort Sumter lying somnolent in the pale, soft sunshine.

Abruptly, your reverie – as if it were a soap bubble – is obliterated by a sudden jolt. Standing with his back to you and looking in the same direction as you, sharing the seascape, is a man who has become the victim of your pedestrian "failure to keep a proper lookout." You blurt apologies.

He answers with something that sounds like: "Arm gley chew weren't runnin."

"Sir?" you ask.

He repeats his statement.

"Sir?" you ask again.

"Cane che unnerstan what arm sane or are you hod of herring?" he asks you.

(*Editor's Note:* Translated into Virginianese, the above statements would be – "I'm glad you weren't running," and "Can't you understand what I'm saying, or are you hard of hearing?")

If you ever visit Charleston, South Carolina and have trouble understanding one of the natives of the "Holy City," you may be asked the above question. But do not be dismayed – neither be downcast or disheartened, for help is at hand in the form of a *Dictionary of Charlestonese.*

Most South Carolinians, and many non-residents of that state, are familiar with the charm and beauty

Dock Street Theatre – *This building was originally the Planter's Hotel. The original theatre opened in 1736 on this same street which at that time was named Dock Street.*

of 300-year-old Charleston. There is also a charm possessed by the people and their inimitable language.

The people have been described as aristocratic, or in the same vein, snobbish, but for the most part they are found to be both friendly and pleasant. To become acquainted with Charlestonians you must talk to them, of course, and in order to comprehend everything they are saying you must be able to understand their "pure and clear accent."

The phrase enclosed in quotations is lifted from the foreword of Ford Ashley Cooper's *Dictionary*

St. Michael's Episcopal Church – *This church was begun in 1752 and and its bells have crossed the Atlantic Ocean five times. George Washington and Lafayette both worshipped here when they visited Charleston.*

of Charlestonese. This compendium of Charlestonese words has been compiled by Frank B. Gilbreth, columnist and assistant publisher of Charleston's *The News and Courier*. Mr. Gilbreth writes under the pen name of Ashley Cooper – the name being taken from the two rivers that flow through and around Charleston.

When "sloppy talkers" like you and me visit the "Holy City" we sometimes complain of having trouble understanding the "perfect English" spoken by Charlestonians. So, for our benefit this eight-page dictionary was published. Herewith is a sampling:

ABODE – Wooden plank.

ARM – I am.

BALKS – A container, such as a match balks.

CAUGHT – A little bed.

DOLLAR – Less sharp, i.e., "My knife was dollar than his own."

FARE – To be a-scairt, i.e., "I fare it may rene, snow and heel."

ICE COOL – The institution of learning which stands midway between grammar school and college.

LACK – Enjoy, i.e., "I lack fried chicken."

PAUNCH – Blow struck with the fist.

TOYED – Something that ebbs and flows off the Bottry.

VERSION – The kind of queen Queen Elizabeth I was.

It is interesting to note that more than one editorial writer has begun columns with words or phrases written with "Charleston" pronunciation. Charlestonese is unique in its diversified roots. It is a

Old Slave Mart Museum – This building was originally a firehouse and later was used as offices of one of the slave auctioneers with slaves being auctioned from the balcony. The building now houses Negro arts and crafts.

curious mixture of English (almost cockney), French and Gullah – that dialect peculiar to the Negroes of the sea islands and low country of South Carolina and Georgia. These three groups were the early inhabitants of the city but there was a large influx of Irish settlers in the 1700's and Germans in the 1800's and these latter groups added their flavoring to the language.

Catfish Row (Cabbage Row) – *Once a Negro alley, this street was called Cabbage Row because vegetables were sold there. It inspired the setting for the Heyward-Gershwin operetta "Porgy and Bess" in which the street was called Catfish Row. This particular building now houses specialty shops.*

Copies of the *Dictionary of Charlestonese* may be obtained by sending 25 cents to *The News and Courier*, Charleston, South Carolina. Proceeds go to the newspaper's Christmas charity, the Good Cheer Fund.

1981 The article that was published in the *New Dominion Magazine* of the *Daily Press* issue of Sunday, March 22, 1970 was the result of our first visit to Charleston.

A few years later I made a second visit there when an older couple, friends, asked me if I would accompany them. They were going to visit his daughter and wanted someone younger along, as well as someone to do the necessary night driving. Because I was eager to visit Charleston again, I readily agreed.

The night driving there and back was not what you would call delightful, but my time spent in Charleston was. And I will always remember the evening that my host family's neighbor and friend – whom I knew also from Virginia – hosted an oyster roast.

A four-foot-by-eight-foot sheet of plywood was laid over saw horses and we circled it, a work glove on one hand, a shucking knife in the other, and a cold beer in front of us. A big washtub of roasted oysters was dumped onto the middle of the makeshift table and we had at them, our shucking knives flashing. We spent the next couple of hours laughing, talking, quaffing cold beer and slurping those delicious, succulent bivalves.

While there I visited the historic part of Charleston for the better part of a day on my own, and was moved to write a poem about the experience. It languished in my files for some years until the *Daily Press* began publishing selective poetry from its readers each Sunday.

The following poem appeared in the "InnerViews" section of the *Daily Press* on November 15, 1981.

"Charleston"

I trod the brick and stone-paved streets
And walked into yesterday,
The month was of November
Though the sun was out of May.
The courtyards and the narrow streets
Held me enthralled and in their sway
I drank the sights of Charleston –
As I walked into yesterday.

The time was then and I was there
Though only for a day,
I paused to breathe the salty air
That coursed down shaded alleyways.
Then Rainbow Road before my eyes,
It drew and held my gaze,
And as I looked I realized
That what I saw was yesterday.

With legs grown numb and senses gorged
I walked out of yesterday,
Past moss and magnolia and the Battery –
Past history on display.
Wrought iron and piazzas I bade goodbye,
In the past I could not stay,
But I know today that on some tomorrow
I will walk again into yesterday.

A. C. H.

A Visit To The Cathedral Bell Tower

September 22, 1974

On the last Saturday of September will occur what is usually a once-a-year event: a climb up winding gothic stairways coupled with a lift in a modern elevator to where you are able to actually look down on the United States Capitol and even the Washington Monument. It is a conducted tour of the Gloria In Excelsis central tower of the Cathedral Church of Saint Peter and Saint Paul. This is the cathedral of the Episcopal Diocese of Washington and so is known as the Washington Cathedral, and often referred to as the National Cathedral because of its ministry on behalf of all churches.

Many articles, including some in local newspapers, have been written about the National Cathedral. Brochures, a quarterly magazine, *Cathedral Age*, and even a book, *A Guide To Washington Cathedral*, have also been published. In addition, there is a Peninsula Chapter of the National Cathedral Association, which has representatives in all Peninsula Episcopal churches. So this soaring and awe-inspiring Gothic edifice is not an unknown structure, as the approximately half-million annual visitors attest. But the aforementioned tour – as its infrequency indicates – is relatively unknown.

This June 25 there was an exception made to the once-a-year rule

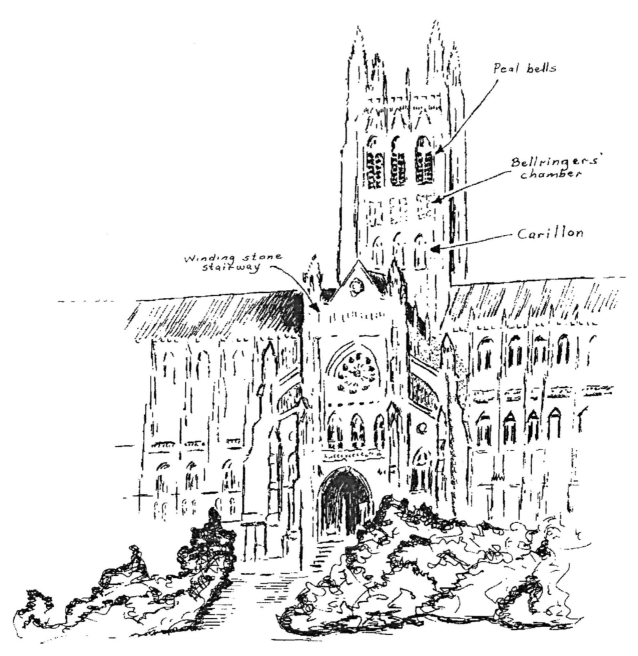

Peal bells

Bellringers' chamber

Carillon

Winding stone stairway

*A sketch of the **National Cathedral**.*

regarding the Tower tour. On that Tuesday afternoon approximately 350 members of the American Guild of English Handbell Ringers, Inc. (A.G.E.H.R., Inc.) – people of all ages – were allowed to ascend the narrow, winding stone stairway that seemed to reach up for miles, and then be lifted, six or eight at a time, in an elevator that took four minutes to reach its destination, which was the topmost room of

the Cathedral. And therein they would view the ten-bell ring, or peal bells, used in the ancient art of change ringing.

On the way up, the elevator would pass the room holding the 53-bell carillon and above that the bell ringers' chamber.

When the elevator stopped and the doors opened the visitors stepped out into the bell chamber and from there, near the top of the 301-foot Tower, they looked down on Washington DC, spread out before them in the hazy summer afternoon.

The Cathedral reposes on Mount St. Alban, itself 400 feet above sea level, and thus the claim that the Tower is the highest point in Washington.

The 10 bronze peal bells in the "Ring," cast by the Whitechapel Bell Foundry in London, England, and dedicated in 1964 on Ascension Day, are mounted on oak frames and moved

The tourists wait patiently for the bell tower elevator.

100

by wooden wheels turned by ropes which hang down into the room below. Mounted in a circle, the bells vary in size from two feet, four inches to four feet, seven inches, and range in weight from 608 pounds to almost 3600 pounds, for a combined weight of nearly seven tons! When they are all rung at once, as they were on New Year's Eve, the Tower literally – and noticeably, although safely – reels from the percussion.

Descending a spiral steel staircase through the thick cement floor, the tourists enter the room below where the ringers of the bells stand in a circle, each with "sally" in hand. A "sally" is the cushioned portion of the rope that the ringer grips.

"...it takes years to really become a proficient bell ringer," one young man is saying in answer to a question by one of those already in the room.

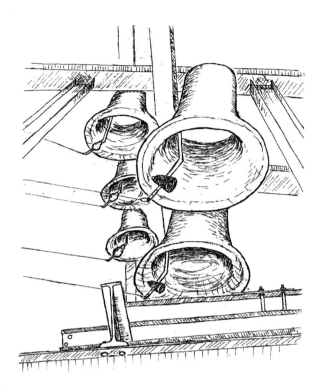

The 53 bells are bolted to beams, tier on tier.

A young lady bell ringer states that most of them have been ringing for from two to five years, and adds that they usually ring twice a week, and also for weddings, etc.

"And you know," the young man interjects, "Paul Revere was a bell ringer and thus had keys to the church. That's how they could get into the Old North Church and hang those lanterns."

Descending the spiral staircase again they reach the chamber containing the 53-bell carillon, a magnificent instrument made by the John Taylor Company of Loughborough, England, a foundry that has been active since the Fourteenth century. Installed during the summer of 1963 and dedicated September 22 of that year, the

A guide demonstrates how to ring a peal bell. They are mounted on wooden wheels which turn as the ropes are pulled.

carillon is played from a manual and pedal keyboard located in "the playing cabin" on the floor of the bellchamber. The bells, ranging in weight from 17 pounds to 12 tons, do not swing because they are bolted rigidly to their supporting beams. When the carillonneur depresses a key or pedal, a wire pulls the clapper to make it hit the inner surface of the bell.

The four largest bells are suspended around the "cabin" and the rest are ranged, tier on tier, above it.

There is still one more descent to make on the spiral staircase and this puts the visitors in the huge chamber where they caught the elevator. There is still a long line waiting to get on.

They are told they are now over 100 feet above the marble floor of the crossing, that point where the transepts (arms) of the Cathedral cross the nave (longest part). (The Cathedral is built in the shape of a cross).

They leave the chamber above the crossing, walk a wooden walkway across the top of the north transept, and look at the top of the vaulted ceiling fall away from beneath either side of the walkway. At the end of the walkway they step out onto a balustrade and blink as they look north toward Maryland. Four steps along the balustrade and the English bell-ringers reenter the Cathedral, wend their way down more stone steps and reach the north balconies. This is where some of the audience will sit later during the program, a one-hour concert of massed handbell ringing that will be performed by twenty-five separate groups. The groups, for the most part, hailed from Delaware, Maryland, the District of Columbia, Virginia and North Carolina but some were there from Michigan, Ohio, Pennsylvania and the Virgin Islands.

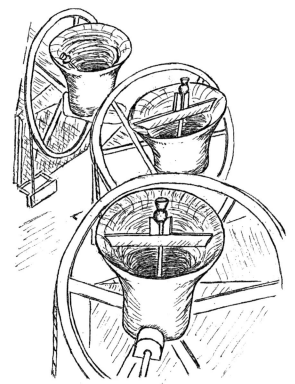

The peal bells in the "Ring" are mounted and moved by wooden wheels turned by ropes.

Off and on for two days they rehearsed, and the handbell concert was the culmination of the 1974 Area iii Festival of the A.G.E.H.R., Inc., and was performed in conjunction with the Washington Cathedral's Summer Festival of programs.

Anyone planning to take the annual Tower tour that is to open to the public should possess stamina and be prepared for standing, walking, and climbing. They should also arrive at the cathedral well before the 11:00 a.m. starting time. Even without the Tower tour, however, a visit to the Cathedral is an unforgettable experience.

THANKS AND CREDITS | *I want to acknowledge* the late Mrs. Frances B. Latimer, Publisher, Hickory House, Eastville, Virginia, and her encouragement. Mrs. Latimer was in publishing in New York City, but some years ago returned to her native Eastern Shore because her elderly, ailing mother needed her.

Mrs. Latimer had plans to publish this collection. However, before she could actually do so, her diseased liver required that she have a transplant. Just prior to Thanksgiving, 2010, she succumbed to complications following the transplant in an Atlanta hospital.

Fortunately, I later learned of Parke Press and Marshall McClure. Her intelligence, enthusiasm, experience and knowledge made this book a reality. I am in her debt.

* * *

As far as I could ascertain when they were quoted, the poems "The Nameless Grave" by Longfellow, and "Newport News" by Miller, are in the public domain. I have not checked on the lyrics to "Newport News Blues" but assume that after all these years those lyrics are, as well.

The rights to "A Special Song for Wanda," written by Don and Harold Reid, were later sold by The Statler Brothers to Universal Music Publishing Company. However, when this article regarding the songs and poems of Newport News was originally written, Don and Harold Reid gave me written permission to quote the lyrics.

The lyrics to "Was a Sunny Day," by Paul Simon, not part of the original article, are owned by:
Simon & Schuster Subsidiary Rights Department
1230 Avenue of the Americas
New York, New York 10020-1513.

A.C.H.

With the Lord's blessing, the writing still goes on, thankfully, and occasionally a drawing is done. "Still a player; still in the game."

Allan C. Hanrahan was born in North Carolina and reared on the Peninsula, where he lived before moving to Smithfield in 1991. He graduated from Newport News High School (Class of '55), the NASA Apprentice School and Christopher Newport College, earning a B.A. in English, with a minor in history – including art history – followed by graduate study at George Washington University in information technology. Mr. Hanrahan retired from NASA, having served in electronics, planning, and as a writer/editor in the Office of Public Affairs; for 22 years he authored the "Personnel Profiles" column in the NASA-LaRC Langley Researcher. Post-NASA he became a substitute school  teacher and then middle school tutor before beginning to freelance for the *Oyster Pointer*. Over the years he has contributed articles – many with drawings – to the *Daily Press*, and reviewed books for that publication, as well as for *The Virginian-Pilot*. Mr. Hanrahan continues to do pen-and-ink drawings, and for the years 2010–2013 his work appeared in the venerable calendar published by The Woman's Club of Smithfield, Inc.

The writings in this work reflect Mr. Hanrahan's Irish heritage and the desire to tell stories, as well as his ties to the Peninsula that extend back to his great-grandfather George Tyler Hanrahan's participation as a Confederate Private in the Battle of Dam Number One, in what is now the Newport News City Park. Those ties continued when his grandfather, George Byron Hanrahan, pastored Second Presbyterian Church 1911–1914, years when his father, Byron Snyder Hanrahan, sold newspapers on Washington Avenue. The family returned to Newport News in 1941 when Allan's father, a World War I veteran of the U.S. Army, began working in the hull design department of the Newport News Shipbuilding and Dry Dock Company as his part of the civilian effort during World War II.

From 1941 onward, the buildings of the Peninsula have been a part of Allan Hanrahan's life, and beginning in the mid-Sixties – as time and circumstances permitted – he has captured as many as he could before they were done away with. He believes that structures are more than the materials that go into their construction; they are imbued with the spirits of those who have lived or worked within their walls.

CPSIA information can be obtained at www.ICGtesting.com
Printed in the USA
BVOW05s1147300114

343104BV00002B/4/P